foreword

to all those who have
been silenced,
the women who
came before me

to my darling reader,

i sit here this 29th of august at 10:43 pm, the underside of a 2006 laptop warming my thighs and silent tears clouding my vision.

yes, i just wrote a frickin' book.

the girl who wrote it feels youthful, naive, almost childish now. having seen more, done more, and met many more, since the beginning of this journey. she loved, she was loved, she hurt, she was hurt, and she lived it all.

from writing fictitious stories about the northern lights at the age of seven or writing my first poems about an aching heart at 13, this trek has been nothing short of spectacular, dreadful, emotional, and weathering (in all the best ways).

i wrote these poems in both the darkest times, when the monsters in my mind roared at their powerful peak and the best of them, when i finally understood what it meant to have butterflies in your tummy, experiencing the kind of happiness that is momentary but long-lasting.

and in said process my lioness grew, she came to life and stepped into her soul.

before you begin, a story for your digesting.

a lioness returns from her hunt to find her
baby cub lifeless, the light in his eyes no
longer shimmering.

to us, human beings, we take such tragedy and
we mourn, we suffer, and we honour in sorrow.
but this lioness, with other mouths to feed and
other days to get through, lets the carcass sit
and walks away.

no funeral is given, no service to commemorate.

all she gets in return for the loss of her
beloved being is a reality check, the circle of
life.

this does not mean she doesn't feel but rather
she cries on the inside, like the rest of her
kin. her exterior remains stoic, protective,
and impassive. although her interior is a
reflection of her inability to demonstrate said
grief, a true identifier of her despair.

in more ways than one i believe we can all
relate to this lioness. wearing an
all-convincing mask to the rest of the world,
while on the inside we shed the ugly kind of
tears. some may be better at concealing it than
others but we all have these moments, hiding
what truly bothers us for the sake of others,
and in turn inconveniencing ourselves and our
oh-so-important state of mental health.

but now in difference, it has come time to discuss these moments, regardless of the good, the bad, and the ugly. and i'm hoping this title will be a good conversation starter.

we are all lionesses. wear it proudly,

-c

predatory

[love stories, human connection,
self-assertion, creation]

it started flowing

from underneath my fingertips

my veins, the arteries

never coerced

rather smooth and tranquil

almost necessary

necessary to my peace

necessary to my sanity

necessary to my being

with fear of being pent up

to explode once past the rim

for keepsake?

not so sure

but to love just who i am

i remember meeting you

and i remember liking you

but i don't remember

going from mutual friends

to platonic soulmates

potted flowers lean towards the light

just as i'm inclined to you

petals reaching for the light

as my arms reach up for you

crazy.

that in this moment

at this time

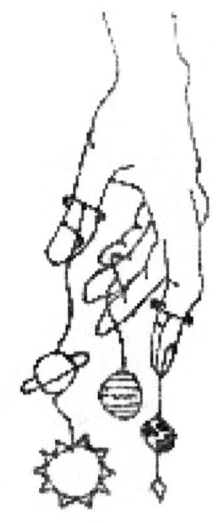

in this universe

we ended up together.

amongst the safety of each other's shadows

we remain hidden,

secluded,

beneath moonlight lurking

until

our footsteps are traced back to

their true owners

love:

notoriously known for
simultaneously making
lives and ruining them
at the same time

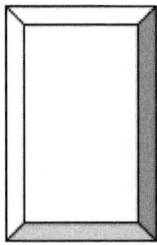

i studied you as if a painting

all the edges, the curves

no longer a mass of flesh and bone

but of discreet uplifting corners 'round the mouth

no longer calling that a smile

but simply

a work of art

he told me i was beautiful

...but

there was always a -but-

if my clothes weren't as "covering"

if i wasn't as smart, as funny

but...

then i met you

who supported my being chilly

embraced what i knew

and laughed when you thought i was

...well...

funny

-*thank you*

if we don't practice it in times
of fulfillment, how will we thrive
in times of emptiness

if my mind grew flowers

and my heart blew them out

would your love be the same

or would you carry doubt

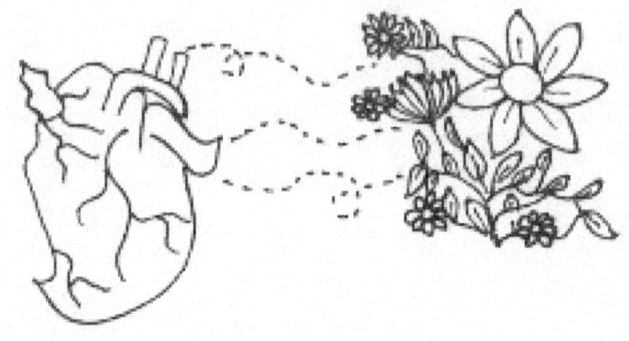

buzzing blistering butterflies

is this what happiness feels like?

those teeny tiny moments

we look upon afterwards

are the very best kind of déja-vous

i remember our walks, of all things. it
could be below freezing, and only in
t-shirts, we'd step outside. hand in hand.
as long as we were connected, the heat of
our bodies would keep the hypothermia away.
illuminated only by the light of glistening
light posts against the snow, our smiles
were bright enough to pave the way.
our breath, fading away into smoke matched
what blew from the butt of your cigarette. a
puff, a word, a laugh and the steam escaped
your lips. the same lips on mine moments
ago.
but we'd keep walking
faster and faster
like the thoughts in our minds, like the
feet carrying our bodies (chilled to the
bone)
back to your house
and when we'd step inside, a wave of warm
air would greet us…
along with our senses
and the chills left me,
almost as fast as you did

to you, a neglectful eye, these are just words, sentences, mushy thoughts. but to me, a naked eye, this is my blood, my sweat, my tears
my art.

the rush drew me in
the bustle, the hurry
the need to go, to get

but perhaps what intrigued me most was
the distraction
the distraction from the emotions
to feel and hurt forgotten

when you have places to be
places to see
that aren't solely within me

you loved like waves
inconsistent and crashing
but i stood at the seaside
waiting and watching

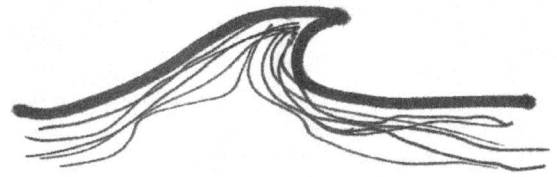

what was he like?

before all of this

how bright was his smile

how full was his laugh

they say i have his eyes

but i'd die for even half his spirit

-*grandpa w.calver*

this is my pollution

these words spilling from the seams of my lips

intoxicating those who take the slightest sip

we are all "real" women

whatever that even means

because the transgender female
who supports and spreads love to her peers,

is more of a woman
than the non-inclusive cisgender one
will ever be

it's those bottomless feelings
that fill me to the brim

the recounting of a memory or
photograph invites the monsoons

back.

when someone extends their love for someone else
it doesn't mean they love you any less.

-destruction of jealousy

we
are
all
sorta
delusional

most
of
us
come
around

what flows from the depths of within me
will not be something i cover in shame
nor is it something i'll hide for your convenience

while something you shun allows life itself
it is something i've been taught to consider a
burden.

but girls, while you sit there with your legs
awkwardly crossed
with your darkest washed jeans
with contraptions inside your body

think of the power and magic you are curating
and bringing to humanity
if you one day so choose

ironic.

losing you was growth for myself

i don't think you understand
and you likely never will
but i'm still madly in love with you
more than i ever was
over the course of our relationship

so maybe i'm madly in longing
desperately wanting your fingers
intertwined in mine
yearning your body holding me close
but madly in longing i'll stay

but to make
the omelette
you have to
break a couple
eggs in the process

turns out that was all i needed
a night out on the town
surrounded by madness
so that i could get away from the chaos around me

i was
nostalgic
on a moment
i was still living

the ever-present road block;

time

carrying the anticipation

wishing there was less

or over-doing your stay

and wishing you had more

two scenarios

one constant

what does it mean to feel alive?
to feel the blood pumping
coursing through every artery and vein

or is it the opposite
not having to worry about the circulation
and instead just living until one day it all
stops

you can run.

away and on to the next girl.

but no matter how fast you go,

you will never escape me.

whether you like it or not,

i am,

and always will be,

a part of you.

a part of your body,

that used to love me unconditionally

a part of your mind,

that tortured me so

and a part of your soul,

that left me in a heartbeat

on your break from other girls
i was your attempt at decaf
but what's worse is you made sure i knew
that i'd never be amount to them
my lack of caffeine
quickly become a loss on your behalf

and there we stood

appreciating the beauty in the stars

but little did you know

i was appreciating the beauty in you

i had to go

i no longer wanted to feel

like the incomplete puzzle

you left my soul

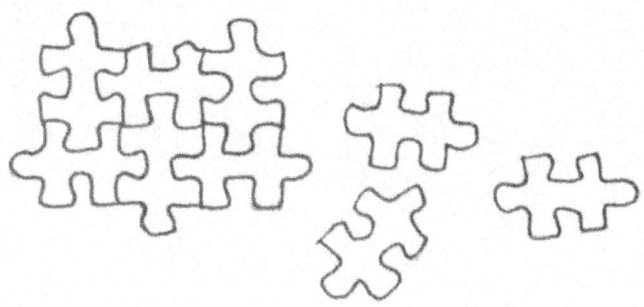

don't get too close,
she'll turn you into a poem

i spent too much precious time
and energy apologizing
on your behalf

to take your weak "i'm sorry"
to heart

that's the thing with war,

you can kill a lot of people

who you think are the problem

but they always come back

you can't kill ideas

nos nez se retrouvent dans la noirceur

les deux seuls au monde

accompagnant nos mots en sourdine

puis à moitié endormi

tu me le dit ...

-bisou d'eskimo

prey

[an achy-breaky heart, emotional growth,
healing, perseverance]

why behind closed doors do i weep? i cried.
but as soon as i'm outside i smile
i deserve an oscar for the emotions that i hide
these feelings that i bury down in piles

with a single word

my heart is shred to pieces

with that single dreaded word

the wolves draw to attack

in those simple seven letters

i fear it's form forever

g o o d b y e

which was i running from?

the world or it's ending

my insides boiling
my heart threatened to jump out of my chest
through gritted teeth
i mutter "yes"

list of things i wanted to hear:

- " i love you "
- " i will never leave "
- " i promise "

imagine feeling so far gone

past the point of no return

having passed that exit a good half hour ago

too accurate to be funny

her laugh was full, mine was empty

the room was still
i heard her call
the ringing of the phone
and then his recorded voicemail
followed by her silent
-but no less present-
tears

you don't deserve to know your influence

not now

you don't deserve the impact on my art

not now

but you got it

hence my creation

my stomach gutted
knowing i was powerless
something entirely out of my control
but you live and you learn
so i learnt how to live

i hate it.

hands laced in fingers to which

you wouldn't trust a trigger

the man of your dreams

turn to men of reality

it's disappointing
we'll never be the way we used to

your smile -

mist

your hugs -

ghostly

your presence -

gone

my finger hovering there
above the caller id with your name
something yearning to pick up the phone and call
despite the advisory of anyone i spoke to

it's a bad idea they said
don't do it they said

ring. ring. ring.

fishing in murky waters
allowing slivering sunlight to pass through
mentalities beaming
minds constantly scheming
While silent raindrops flew

yes.

i ended it

but along with this finale

came my own heartbreak of sorts

including my realization

of wanting you back

paper cuts suck.

that's all

i'm tired.

tired of

reciting my mirror-rehearsed explanations
to you turned back

tired of

defending myself through
a phone number i know you've blocked

because my sweet melodies are now
for those who dare to listen
and your ears
are forever plugged

officer,

i'm trying to remember

but i completely disassociated

upon commission of the deed

my soul left my body

leaving my subconscious to deal with the

situation

the rest of me to pick up the pieces after

i am the frog in the pot
the frog who'll be coaxed
into staying over due
thrown into bearable circumstances
but sticks around until it's all too much

too real

too late

while the frog isn't aware of
the boiling water encapsulating him
i'm not aware of the boiling water
encapsulating me

i think it's insane

that after all this time

you still can't understand.

yes, life will take its course

off-roading every once and again

but your derailment

has had a chain reaction

on countless dragged-in people

the room entirely empty
i was suffocating on my own fumes
strong. powerful. relentless.
blocking my eyes, ears, nose in opposition
but flooding couldn't be kept at bay

please stop.

please.

you're making it harder to forget you.

you can't come back
once you've pulled the trigger
my triggers.
the words spitting out like roulette
striking me like gunshots

my insides boiling
my heart threatened to jump out of my chest
through gritted teeth
i mutter "yes"

i'm really hoping here
to have the power
to suppress what i don't want arisen

moving quickly to another

who's next you always ask

a constant flow, a swapping system

of humans, rather, ideologies

because as humans we miss ideas

hence your claim of missing me

you bruised my soul
just like you hurt
my hands and knees
from pleading

i spoke so loud
began to shout
the world was silent
pushed me out

everything went dark at once
my thoughts were cloudy, started to jump
but i stood still shaking the gun
until you told me to get up and run

the crackle of a laugh through

the phone

missing the real thing so very much

with bad service

it sounds fractured

cut off from the rest of the world

or maybe just from me

counting down the days now

thirty-two too long now

but only two left

the jokes piled in my mind

wanting desperately to hear that laugh

now.

don't worry, they're only pixels
were her famous last words
as she went under digital control
of someone else
tied by the wrists of the cables
from her controller

i let it slide

your hand on my waist

i let it slide

your exhausting commentary

i let it slide

your controlling mannerism

i let it slide

don't let it slide.

you're scared of commitment

yet you're the repercussion

of the heart on my ribcage

but that's the thing, i'm not like you

because i would never be able to
do that to her

not in the darkest hours
of my darkest days

i'm
broken

i jolt awake
did i imagine her?
the ever present source
of laughter, safety, grace
bound forever at the fingertips
pursued the art of magic
performed the disappearing trick

was it faux-happiness

wanting to see in something

that wasn't there

loving the idea of it

but never the real thing

i don't think i'll ever find out

i used to call myself the wild girl
the feral, untamed friend
later realizing it had been a mask
put on to show others that i,
but not my feelings,
could fool around
and get untangled

you have to retrain your
mind to see the beauty
and the power within
yourself

i know it's hard

trust me

but when you allow
yourself to fall into
the arms of that process

it gets easier

i promise

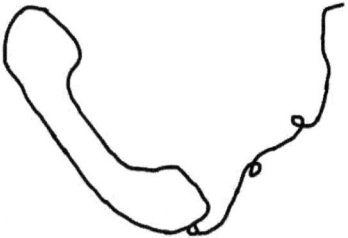

beep. panic. hang up

it was always he said, he said

because she never spoke

i picked it out
stripped it completely to the bone
as my mother, grandmother and sisters had
done before me
wiped it away with every tweezed eyebrow
mentally deleted it with every waxed leg
and rethreaded my outlook with every
whitened tooth

because what i'd adopted had been there too
long
what i subconsciously accepted was wrong
and even if i tried it shouldn't belong

but there it was
embedded into centuries of work
deeply rooted into culture overdue

and i had to reverse it
to and for myself
to and for my other women

because unpicking my own misogyny was the
becoming of my own womanhood

i implore you
please
grind me down to nothing

until the marrow of my bones
is splattered on the floor

my body empty of what it needs

but my mind far more
sparse

quick
clean up the mess
these teardrops shant be seen

help
clean up my mess
these teardrops never should have been

flickering them across my vision
as stars do to a sky

but i promise you
these teardrops are not mine

her eyes
glistening oh so bright with embers
reflected only the purest retreat
the moon rising
initiating truest forms of night
rose with our hopes of recovery
preaching survival of the fittest
for our oh so fitting gal

did you even catch her name?
before you had her drink your poison
throwing her into worlds of pain
with elegance and nonchalance forgotten

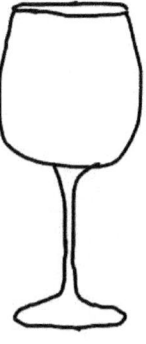

she was both my favourite
and most hated
person

more of a memory
at this point

but i think i just hated the fact
that i couldn't stop
loving her

you stared me down

with eyes fiercer than medusa

like the snakeskin i couldn't shed

and my heart momentarily stone

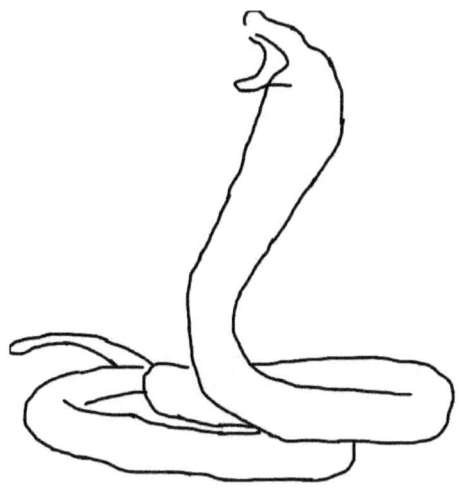

i devoured your words

as if i hadn't eaten in days

to my darling reader,

i sit here this 5th of september at 9:54 pm,
the underside of a 2006 laptop warming my
thighs and silent tears clouding my vision.

yes, i just wrote a frickin' book.

but now, contrary to the version of yourself
having read my little foreword, you've come to
the end of a winding, steep road in my head,
also known as my train of emotions.

and i'd like to say thank you.

thank you to you, having made my dream
possible, in having someone actually interested
in reading what i have to write and taking
pleasure in understanding my messy messy brain.
i'm honoured. truly.

-*thank you thank you thank you*

this process wouldn't have been possible
without the very generous help of a few
particular people, and for that they need some
recognition. or should i say acknowledgments
(*wink wink*)(sorry that was an awful attempt
at a transition to the acknowledgement section,
coming right up)

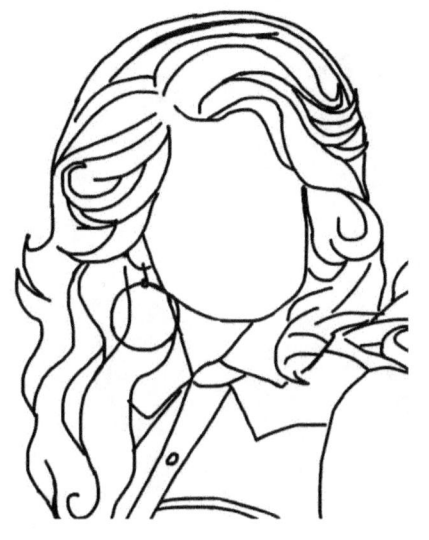

d o l l y   p a r t o n

"i was the first woman to burn my bra - it took the fire department four days to put it out"

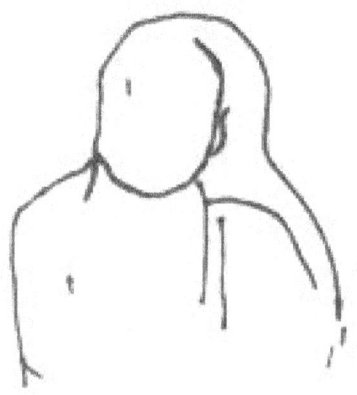

i n d y

"i like my country music at a volume where i
can't hear you complaining about it"

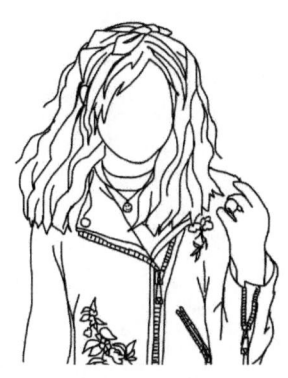

k a y

"i wish i had disney transition music irl
except it would just be welcome to my life
by simple plan"

(and a special thank you for helping me out
with some illustrations, you're a mega cool
gal)

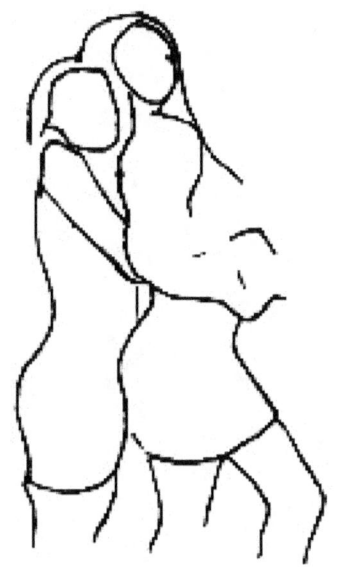

c a s s i d y

"i need my tums"

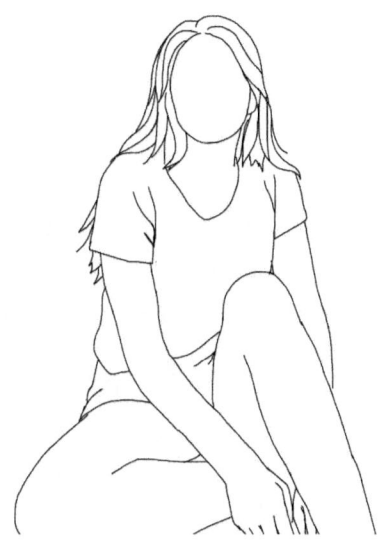

d i a n a

"did you guys watch survivor? well there
goes my conversation starter"

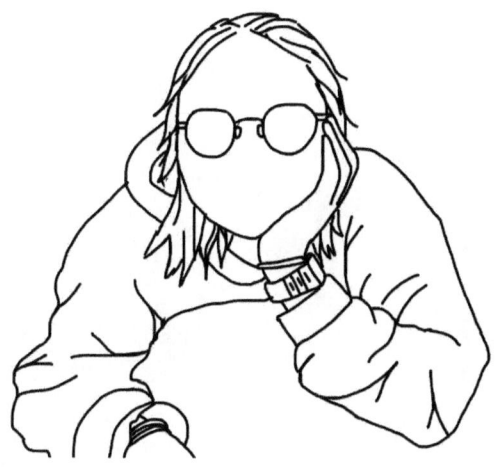

si qi

"genuinely"

(your heart is massive dude,
and i love ya for it)

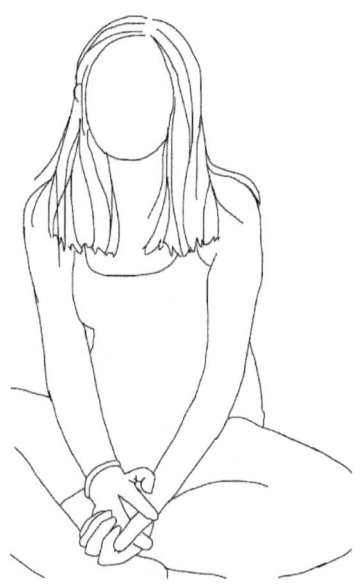

v i c t o r i a

"billy idol is the superior billy"

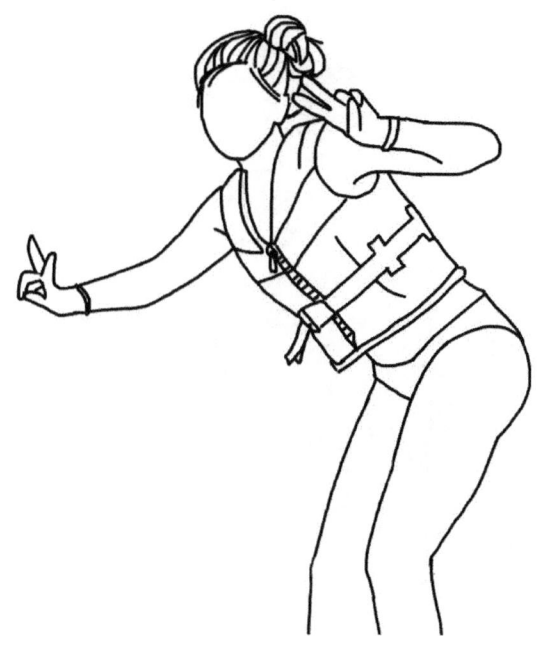

k a t

"no baby no"

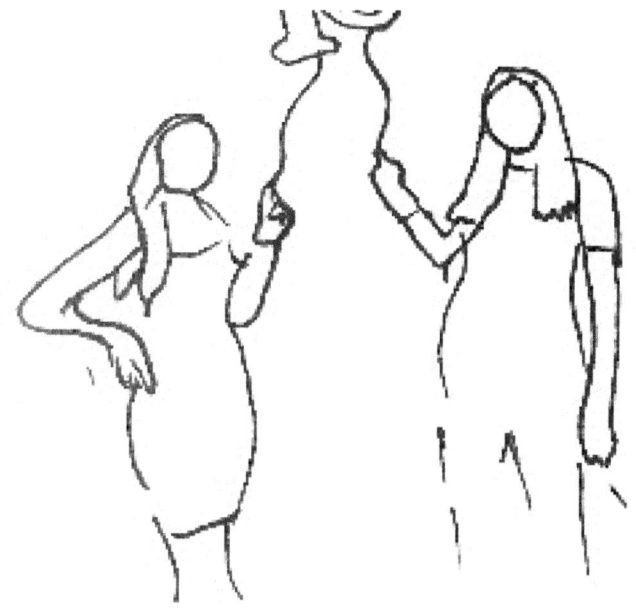

k a t i e

"you are guac babygirl"

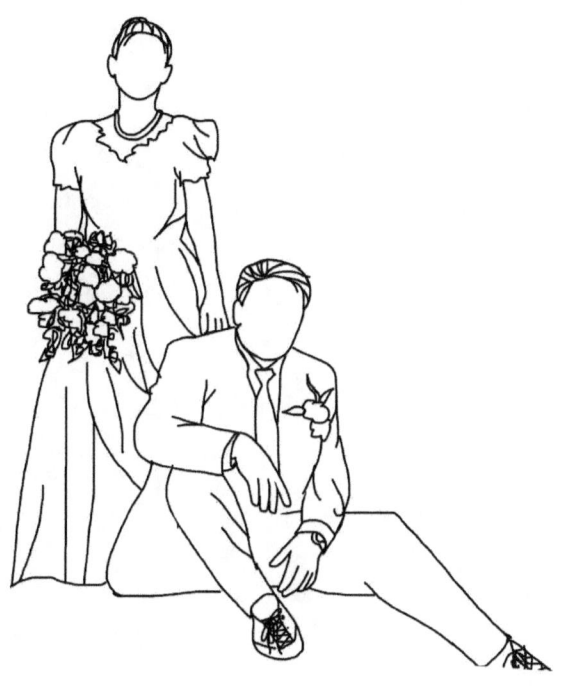

m a m a & d a d d y

"maybe"
(which i've learnt over time means no)

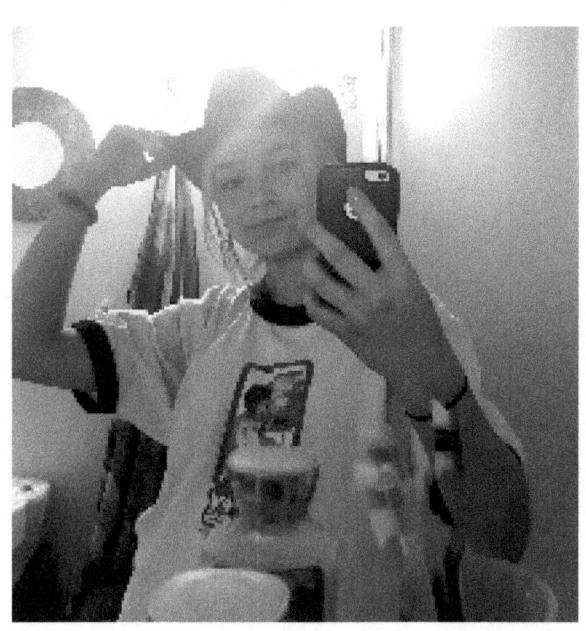

about the author

cordelia jamieson's life
is as pictured above.
trying on cowboy hats
just for fun, brushing
her teeth and enjoying
some good ol' bob ross.
Oh yeah, and she likes
to write sometimes :)

www.ingramcontent.com/pod-product-compliance
Lightning Source LLC
Chambersburg PA
CBHW072135170526
45158CB00004BA/1388